W9-BVQ-016

FREDERICK COUNTY PUBLIC LIBRARIES

CAUSE AND EFFECT

FOR *Life* AND LIBERTY

CAUSES AND EFFECTS

of the **Declaration of Independence**

BY BECKY LEVINE

Consultant:
Benjamin L. Carp, PhD
Associate Professor of History
Tufts University
Medford, Massachusetts

CAPSTONE PRESS
a capstone imprint

Fact Finders Books are published by Capstone Press,
1710 Roe Crest Drive, North Mankato, Minnesota 56003
www.capstonepub.com

Copyright © 2014 by Capstone Press, a Capstone imprint. All rights reserved.
No part of this publication may be reproduced in whole or in part, or stored in a
retrieval system, or transmitted in any form or by any means, electronic, mechanical,
photocopying, recording, or otherwise, without written permission of the publisher.

Library of Congress Cataloging-in-Publication Data
Levine, Becky.
For life and liberty : causes and effects of the Declaration of Independence / Becky
Levine.
pages cm.—(Cause and effect)
Includes bibliographical references and index.
Summary: "Explains the Declaration of Independence and its impact"—Provided by
publisher.
ISBN 978-1-4765-3931-7 (library hardcover)—ISBN 978-1-4765-5129-6 (paperback)—
ISBN 978-1-4765-5978-0 (eBook pdf)
1. United States. Declaration of Independence—Juvenile literature. 2. United States—
Politics and government—To 1775--Juvenile literature. 3. United States—Politics and
government—1775-1783—Juvenile literature. I. Title.
E221.L48 2014
973.3'13—dc23   2013037019

Editorial Credits
Abby Colich, editor; Kyle Grenz, designer; Svetlana Zhurkin, media researcher;
Jennifer Walker, production specialist

Photo Credits
Alamy: North Wind Picture Archives, 6; Corbis, 12; iStockphotos: huePhotography, 29;
Library of Congress, 5, 9, 11, 16, 19, 20; Line of Battle Enterprise, 14; National Archives
and Records Administration/Our Documents, 26; National Park Service: Harpers
Ferry Center, 23, Colonial National Historical Park/Sidney E. King, 7; Newscom/
Prisma/Album, 10, 21; Shutterstock: Mark Hayes, 25, Susan Law Cain, cover (inset);
SuperStock, cover (middle); Wikipedia: U.S. Capitol, 24

Printed in the United States of America in Stevens Point, Wisconsin.
092013   007769WZS14

Table OF CONTENTS

THE *American* COLONIES

The United States has not always been an independent country. In the 17th and 18th centuries, Great Britain controlled many parts of what is now the United States. British people had moved to North America and formed **colonies**.

Sometimes British rulers didn't pay much attention to the colonies. The colonies were far away—all the way across an ocean. **Colonists** had freedom to do what they wanted. They were happy living this way.

colony—a place that is settled by people from another country and is controlled by that country
colonist—a person who settles in a new territory that is governed by his or her home country

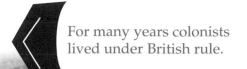

For many years colonists lived under British rule.

Over time things began to change between the colonies and Great Britain. Colonists wanted a say in laws they were being forced to follow. Eventually they wanted to form their own country. In a document called the Declaration of Independence, colonists would announce they no longer considered themselves a part of Great Britain. This document affected the development of the United States in many ways. There were many reasons the colonists wanted to break away from British rule.

Colonists from other countries, including this Dutch family, also wanted freedom from British rule.

settler—a person who makes a home in a new place

Early colonists took land from American Indians to build new communities.

Before British Rule

For thousands of years, American Indians were the only people living in North America. They spread all over the continent, creating their own communities and cultures. European settlers came into conflict with Indians, usually over land. Many Indians died of diseases brought by Europeans. But they kept fighting for their land and still live in North America today.

In the 900s Norse Vikings reached present-day Canada. But they didn't stay for long. After that it was hundreds of years before Christopher Columbus first landed in the Caribbean in 1492. Spanish **settlers** began coming to America in the 1500s. Dutch, French, Welsh, Swedish, and others came too.

In the late 1500s and 1600s, people from Great Britain began sailing to America. Many of them left Great Britain because they wanted more freedom. Some wanted the freedom to practice their religion. Others wanted to own land and make money. Whatever the reason, they all became a part of new communities in the colonies.

What Caused the COLONISTS to Want INDEPENDENCE?

As the population of the colonies grew and spread over more land, colonists wanted to make their own decisions. They argued with Great Britain's leaders about the laws they passed.

Cause #1—New Taxes

From 1756 to 1763 Great Britain fought a war against France on land in and around the colonies. Great Britain won the war, but it cost the country a lot of money.

People living in the colonies worked hard. They sold goods for money. Great Britain wanted some of that money to pay for the war. They wanted to **tax** the colonies. Taxes would make colonists give some of their money to the British **government**.

tax—money collected from a country's citizens to help pay for running the government

government—the group of people who make laws, rules, and decisions for a country or state

Many newspapers protested the Stamp Act by printing a skull and crossbones where the stamp should appear.

Great Britain passed many tax laws that placed taxes on basic goods. The Stamp Act was particularly harsh. Under this law, colonists had to pay tax on all documents and printed materials, including newspapers. The other laws taxed things such as sugar, glass, paint, lead, and tea.

No Taxation Without Representation

People in the colonies wanted "No taxation without representation." Colonists weren't allowed to vote for Great Britain's government. This meant they had no representation in Great Britain. They didn't get to say how Great Britain should use the colonists' tax money. Colonists didn't want to pay taxes to Great Britain any longer. They wanted to decide how to spend their own money.

The Boston Massacre has also been called The Bloody Massacre in King Street.

Cause #2—The Boston Massacre

The British government sent soldiers to the colonies. The soldiers tried to force the colonists to follow Great Britain's laws. On March 5, 1770, a group of about 60 angry colonists gathered in Boston. They threw snowballs and stones at British soldiers. The soldiers fired their guns into the unruly crowd. Five colonists were killed, and six were injured in the Boston Massacre. Many in Boston continued to resent the British soldiers for years afterward.

Cause #3—The Coercive Acts

Colonists didn't want to pay unfair taxes. So they stopped buying certain goods from Great Britain. In 1773 three ships carried tea into Boston Harbor. A group of colonists dressed up as Indians. They went on the boats and threw all the tea into the ocean, destroying it. This event later became known as the Boston Tea Party. Colonists wanted to show the British that their taxes were unfair.

This act caused Great Britain to pass laws that made life even more difficult for the colonists. One law, the Boston Port Bill, closed the port of Boston. Ships couldn't bring food or other goods into Boston. Also, people in Boston couldn't send their own goods to be sold elsewhere. As a result, colonists made less money. They called these new laws the Coercive Acts.

Colonists showed the British how unfair they thought the tea tax was by destroying tea.

Cause #4—The Battles of Lexington and Concord

In 1774 British soldiers took control of Boston. They were still trying to force colonists to obey their laws. On April 19, 1775, British soldiers marched out of Boston into Lexington. Colonists thought they wanted to capture Samuel Adams and John Hancock. They were two of the colonial leaders who wanted to break free from British rule. Then the soldiers planned to go to Concord, where colonists were storing gunpowder. The British soldiers planned to destroy the gunpowder. They were trying to stop the colonists from rebelling.

Colonists battle the British at Concord Bridge in Massachusetts.

patriot—a person who sided with the colonies during the Revolutionary War
loyalist—a colonist who was loyal to Great Britain during the Revolutionary War

The colonists were ready. They found out what the British soldiers were going to do. Horseback riders, including Paul Revere, rode to tell people outside the towns that the soldiers were coming. Adams and Hancock escaped before the soldiers got to Lexington. In both towns colonists got ready to fight.

British soldiers then arrived in Lexington. Great Britain had many more soldiers than the colonists did. The British won the battle, killing seven colonists. They left Lexington to go to Concord. But the colonists weren't done fighting. They stopped the British from going into Concord and attacked the British soldiers as they marched back to Boston. The colonists killed or wounded more than 100 soldiers.

Loyalists for Great Britain

People in the colonies who wanted their own country called themselves **patriots**. Some colonists didn't want independence though. These **loyalists** wanted the colonies to stay part of Great Britain. Many loyalists fought for Great Britain. Others left the colonies. Some of those who stayed were attacked by patriots. Some loyalists had to leave their homes to be safe. They lived and worked in the colonies. After the American Revolution, they became part of the new United States.

Cause #5—The Continental Congress

Each colony had its own local government led by elected leaders. These men made laws for the colonies. But there were 13 colonies, so there were 13 different governments and 13 sets of rules. The colonies had never worked together, and leaders often disagreed. Now, though, they knew the colonies had to unite against Great Britain.

Delegates debate in the Colony of Virginia prior to the Continental Congress.

In September 1774 colonial leaders met in Philadelphia for the First Continental Congress. Some leaders in Congress wanted to be independent from Great Britain. Others wanted to keep talking to Great Britain. They didn't want to fight. The colonies could not agree on one plan. So the leaders sent a letter to Great Britain listing the things colonists wanted Great Britain to do. The letter did not ask for independence.

Britain's King George III ignored the letter. In 1775 the Second Continental Congress met. Colonists were angrier than before. The **delegates** agreed on more things. They formed a Continental army led by George Washington. A year later the delegates declared their independence from Great Britain in the Declaration of Independence.

FAST FACT: Georgia was the only one of the 13 colonies that didn't send a delegate to the First Continental Congress.

delegate—someone who represents other people at a meeting

Thomas Paine

Cause #6—*Common Sense*

Some Americans were ready for independence from Great Britain. But others still wanted to be British. Then in 1776 Thomas Paine wrote a pamphlet called *Common Sense*. In *Common Sense* Paine told Americans to break free from Great Britain. He told them to make their own country. Paine didn't use long sentences or too many big words. Everybody in the colonies could understand his argument. He told them to build their own future. *Common Sense* changed the minds of many colonists. They were ready to take a stand for independence.

"I challenge the warmest advocate for reconciliation, to shew, a single advantage that this continent can reap, by being connected with Great Britain."—*Common Sense*

THE Declaration of INDEPENDENCE

Congress asked John Adams, Benjamin Franklin, Thomas Jefferson, Robert R. Livingston, and Roger Sherman to draft the Declaration. The men shared ideas about what it should say. Then Jefferson wrote the Declaration.

The Declaration of Independence has about 1,300 words. In those words, Jefferson said that the colonies were independent. He listed the colonies' complaints against Great Britain. He said these things were the reason colonists wanted their own country. Jefferson wrote that the colonies were now "The United States of America."

The words in the Declaration of Independence united the 13 colonies in their desire for independence. Jefferson wrote that every man was equal and should have the same rights.

The other four men read what Jefferson had written and made some changes. Jefferson showed the document to Congress. The delegates made more changes. Finally, on July 4, 1776, the first delegates signed the Declaration of Independence.

The men in charge of creating the Declaration of Independence are now known as the Committee of Five.

"We hold these truths to be self-evident, that all men are created equal, that they are endowed by their Creator with certain inalienable Rights, that among these are Life, Liberty, and the pursuit of Happiness."—The Declaration of Independence

In CONGRESS, JULY 4, 1776.

A DECLARATION

BY THE REPRESENTATIVES OF THE

UNITED STATES OF AMERICA,

IN GENERAL CONGRESS ASSEMBLED.

WHEN in the Course of human Events, it becomes necessary for one People to dissolve the Political Bands which have connected them with another, and to assume among the Powers of the Earth, the separate and equal Station to which the Laws of Nature and of Nature's God entitle them, a decent Respect to the Opinions of Mankind requires that they should declare the causes which impel them to the Separation.

We hold these Truths to be self-evident, that all Men are created equal, that they are endowed by their Creator with certain unalienable Rights, that among these are Life, Liberty, and the Pursuit of Happiness—That to secure these Rights, Governments are instituted among Men, deriving their just Powers from the Consent of the Governed, that whenever any Form of Government becomes destructive of these Ends, it is the Right of the People to alter or to abolish it, and to institute new Government, laying its Foundation on such Principles, and organizing its Powers in such Form, as to them shall seem most likely to effect their Safety and Happiness. Prudence, indeed, will dictate that Governments long established should not be changed for light and transient Causes; and accordingly all Experience hath shewn, that Mankind are more disposed to suffer, while Evils are sufferable, than to right themselves by abolishing the Forms to which they are accustomed. But when a long Train of Abuses and Usurpations, pursuing invariably the same Object, evinces a Design to reduce them under absolute Despotism, it is their Right, it is their Duty, to throw off such Government, and to provide new Guards for their future Security. Such has been the patient Sufferance of these Colonies; and such is now the Necessity which constrains them to alter their former Systems of Government. The History of the present King of Great-Britain is a History of repeated Injuries and Usurpations, all having in direct Object the Establishment of an absolute Tyranny over these States. To prove this, let Facts be submitted to a candid World.

He has refused his Assent to Laws, the most wholesome and necessary for the public Good.

He has forbidden his Governors to pass Laws of immediate and pressing Importance, unless suspended in their Operation till his Assent should be obtained;

Spreading the Word

In the 1700s people didn't have phones or TVs. They didn't have the Internet or e-mail. Congress had other ways to tell colonists about the Declaration.

Colonists in Philadelphia found out right away. They rang church bells and fired cannons to celebrate. John Dunlap was a printer in Philadelphia. Congress asked him to make copies. They sent these copies to each colony. People hung copies on buildings. They told the news to friends. Congress sent a copy to George Washington. He had it read to his soldiers, who were actively fighting British troops. Soon everybody knew that the colonies had joined together to become independent from Great Britain.

George Washington's troops heard the Declaration of Independence on July 9, 1776.

What the Declaration Didn't Say

Many colonists owned African-Americans as slaves. When Thomas Jefferson wrote the Declaration of Independence, he wrote that slavery was a very bad thing. He blamed slavery in the colonies on King George. The Continental Congress took these words out of the Declaration. Delegates were afraid too many slave owners wouldn't support the Declaration. The Declaration of Independence said "all men are created equal," but slaves did not have equal rights.

What Effects Did the DECLARATION of INDEPENDENCE HAVE?

The men who signed the Declaration of Independence risked their lives for independence. The effects of the document were many and long-lasting.

Effect #1—The American Revolution

While the Declaration of Independence declared the colonists' freedom from Great Britain, patriots still had to win a war. Great Britain was still trying to force people in America to follow British laws. From 1775 to 1783 colonists fought a war for independence from Great Britain. They fought to make Great Britain accept the colonists' independence.

Great Britain had a huge army. At one time 50,000 British soldiers were in the colonies. When the war started, patriots had fewer than 5,000 soldiers. The British thought they would win the war. But North America was too big for British soldiers to go everywhere they needed to be.

British troops surrender at Yorktown, ending the Revolutionary War.

The colonial army was smaller. But with help from the French, colonists won the war. On October 19, 1781, Great Britain **surrendered** at Yorktown, Virginia. On September 3, 1783, Great Britain signed the **Treaty** of Paris. Great Britain finally recognized the United States of America as an independent nation.

surrender—to give up or admit defeat
treaty—an official agreement between two or more groups or countries

Effect #2–The United States Constitution

The Declaration of Independence said that the United States was its own country. During the war colonies were bound together by the Articles of Confederation. This agreement set rules to follow during the war. But some Americans felt that the new country needed a better system of government.

In May 1787 delegates from every state except Rhode Island came to Philadelphia. They debated "The Great Compromise," which said that each state would be equally represented in the new government.

Delegates sign the Constitution in 1787.

The new **Constitution** said that the United States of America had one main government. This government could make laws for the country. The first sentence of the Constitution is called the Preamble. The Preamble tells people the reason the Constitution was written:

"...to form a more perfect Union, establish Justice, insure domestic Tranquility, provide for the common defence, promote the general Welfare, and secure the Blessings of Liberty to ourselves and our Posterity..."

constitution—the system of laws and powers of the government

Effect #3—Bill of Rights

Some of the delegates thought the Constitution gave the government too much power. They wanted to make sure that people in America still had enough freedom. Some states wouldn't accept the new Constitution unless it included a Bill of Rights. The Bill of Rights made sure that every person had certain rights. These rights cannot be violated when the Congress makes new laws.

Effect #4—A New Government

The Constitution also created three **branches** of government. These branches still exist today. The legislative branch has a Senate and a House of Representatives. They write laws for the United States. The executive branch makes sure that people obey the laws. The president of the United States is the leader of the executive branch. The judicial branch includes the Supreme Court. This court makes sure the laws of the Constitution are upheld.

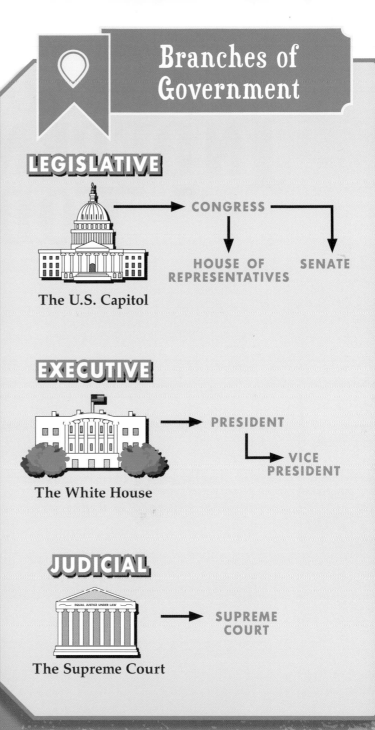

Branches of Government

LEGISLATIVE

The U.S. Capitol

CONGRESS

HOUSE OF REPRESENTATIVES — SENATE

EXECUTIVE

The White House

PRESIDENT

VICE PRESIDENT

JUDICIAL

EQUAL JUSTICE UNDER LAW

The Supreme Court

SUPREME COURT

branch—one of three parts of U.S. government

THE *Declaration* OF INDEPENDENCE TODAY

The Declaration of Independence was signed on July 4, 1776. Today Americans still celebrate this day. Americans consider July 4 the birthday of their country.

The Declaration of Independence remains an important document. Other countries used it as inspiration when declaring their own independence. It was referred to during the **antislavery movement** and the fight for women's rights in the United States. The original copy is at the National Archives building in Washington, D.C. Thousands of people come to view it each year. It is studied as one of the most significant documents in American history.

antislavery movement—work to end slavery throughout the world in the 18th and 19th centuries

Americans have many ways of celebrating Independence Day every July 4.

FAST FACT: Thomas Jefferson and John Adams were two of the men most involved in working for independence and in writing the Declaration of Independence. Both men died on July 4, 1826. The date was 50 years, exactly, after the first member of the Continental Congress signed the Declaration of Independence.

GLOSSARY

antislavery movement (an-ti-SLAY-vur-ee MOOV-muhnt)—work to end slavery throughout the world in the 18th and 19th centuries

branch (BRANCH)—one of three parts of U.S. government

colony (KAH-luh-nee)—a place that is settled by people from another country and is controlled by that country

colonist (KAH-luh-nist)—a person who settles in a new territory that is governed by his or her home country

constitution (kon-stuh-TOO-shuhn)—the system of laws and powers of the government

delegate (DEL-uh-guht)—someone who represents other people at a meeting

government (GUHV-urn-muhnt)—the group of people who make laws, rules, and decisions for a country or state

loyalist (LOI-uh-list)—a colonist who was loyal to Great Britain during the Revolutionary War

patriot (PAY-tree-uht)—a person who sided with the colonies during the Revolutionary War

settler (SET-lur)—a person who makes a home in a new place

surrender (suh-REN-dur)—to give up or admit defeat

tax (TAKS)—money collected from a country's citizens to help pay for running the government

treaty (TREE-tee)—an official agreement between two or more groups or countries

READ MORE

Cunningham, Kevin. *The Massachusetts Colony.* New York: Children's Press, 2012.

Leavitt, Amie Jane. *The Declaration of Independence in Translation: What It Really Means.* Mankato, Minn.: Capstone Press, 2009.

Kerley, Barbara. *Those Rebels, John and Tom.* New York: Scholastic Press, 2012.

Raum, Elizabeth. *The Declaration of Independence.* Chicago: Heinemann Library, 2013.

INTERNET SITES

FactHound offers a safe, fun way to find Internet sites related to this book. All of the sites on FactHound have been researched by our staff.

Here's all you do:

Visit *www.facthound.com*

Type in this code: 9781476539317

Check out projects, games and lots more at
www.capstonekids.com

CRITICAL THINKING USING THE COMMON CORE

1. Before writing the Declaration of Independence, delegates sent a letter to King George III. What if Great Britain had a leader who took into account the colonists' concerns? What might have been different? (Integration of Knowledge and Ideas)

2. Compare and contrast the illustrations on pages 21 and 23. What do you think the two different sets of soldiers were thinking and feeling? (Craft and Structure)

3. How do you think life changed for the average American after the Declaration of Independence, both immediately and in the years following the Revolutionary War? Use evidence from the text to support your answers. (Key Idea and Details)

INDEX

MAY 2014   2 1982 03020 5789